A Harmonious Approach to Working with Dogs

Stacey Manzo, CPDT-KA, CPCFT

Published by:
WagMore U

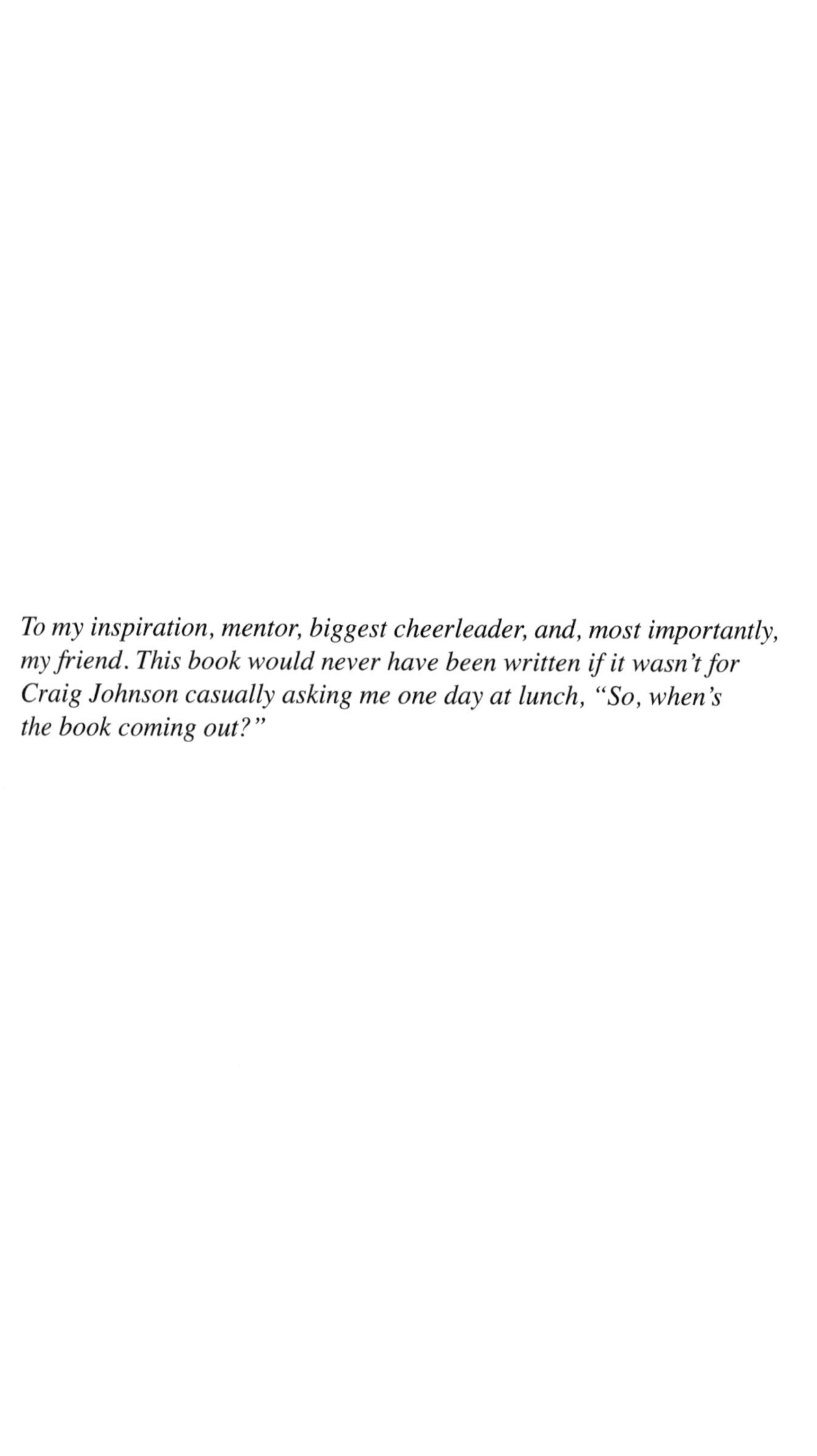

To my inspiration, mentor, biggest cheerleader, and, most importantly, my friend. This book would never have been written if it wasn't for Craig Johnson casually asking me one day at lunch, "So, when's the book coming out?"

Contents

Introduction

"What makes your training methods differ from other dog trainers who have come before you?" my friend asked.

After a brief pause, I summed up my philosophy in one statement: **"It's all about empowering the dog to make choices."**

Unlike traditional training methods, *Confident by Choice* gives your dog a vote. If your dog chooses not to interact with you when you attempt to engage them, respect their decision. Simple as that.

This lack of pressure allows your dog to choose to interact with you on *their* terms. When they do, that means they're comfortable and committed to doing the work you introduce to them. Working with a dog in a relaxed and willing mental state cultivates change much faster. Reliable behavior leads to a more fluid training session, and, best of all, everyone feels good. And who doesn't want that?

These days, I see more and more dogs that struggle to live in the world we humans created for them.

Decades ago, at a time when dogs roamed free, they were well-adjusted and better behaved. In countries where dogs are permitted off leash and roam towns and farms, they seem to be well balanced. For example, in France, dogs are welcome just about everywhere and accepted in most public places which gives the dogs more opportunities for adventures to bust the boredom of being housebound.

While any dog can benefit from this laid-back, more natural approach, pet parents with dogs labeled reactive, fearful, or shy tend to see a profound impact when they leverage *Confident by Choice*—and this is no surprise. By giving your canine companion control over their day-to-day experiences and interactions, you can help them build confidence, resiliency, and trust.

This book will equip you with a new and empathetic approach to dealing with your dog. It will teach you how to read your dog's body language better and support their mental health and happiness through practical examples of incorporating learning moments and trust-building into everyday living.

Many of the lessons you'll learn come straight from dogs I've worked with in the past. As you explore *Confident by Choice*, keep an open mind and see where the journey takes you because your dog's growth path is as unique as your relationship. And that's the way it should be.

Chapter 1

Every Dog Gets a Vote

What does this mean, exactly?

It means giving dogs choices and allowing them to make decisions. According to *Dictionary.com*, vote means "to express or signify will or choice in a matter." But some other definitions capture an aspect of choice that's important in the context of working with dogs: *Collins Dictionary* defines vote as "the right to exercise such a decision or choice."

Many people don't give their dogs the right or opportunity to choose out of fear of being called "soft" or lacking "leadership." They've been duped into believing that they need to assert themselves to become the "alpha" in the relationship. Some pet owners never consider letting Rover vote as an option.

In the book *Paradox of Choice* by Barry Schwartz, he states that Western societies commonly associate a large amount of choice with welfare and freedom. Still, too much choice results in less happiness and less satisfaction and can even lead to paralysis. This occurs when too many choices overwhelm your dog, rendering them unable to make a decision.

In short, having too many options isn't as good as it seems, and the same goes for your dog. In some dogs, too much choice can lead to increased anxiety and poor decision-making. While it's important to create opportunities for your dog to make choices, you need to structure those choices so the outcomes that can follow are positive no matter what your dog decides.

Photo courtesy of Unsplash - Beth Macdonald

This is a delicate balance, but here's a simple way to break it down: we're seeking many opportunities to make choices, not many choices for each opportunity.

The best outcomes occur when a dog's choice is limited to two items or actions. For example, when you're out walking with your dog:

- Do you want to go right or left?
- Would you like to go back to the car or keep walking?
- Want to go for a swim or stay on the path?
- Should we stop in the shade or continue our stroll?

Choices are as simple as deciding which toy to play with, which couch to lie on, and whether to sit or lie down.

Choice as Empowerment: A Lesson from Max

Max, an inquisitive mixed breed rescue dog, was supposed to be an "easy" (read: low maintenance) dog. My client admitted that she didn't have time to devote to training, and she had hoped that Max would ease into her new life. Unfortunately, she adopted a kind and spirited pup who suffered from a recurring medical issue that may have been affecting his behavior because he was in a constant state of pain. After months of medical bills, tons of tears, and frustration, she reached out to me as a last resort.

I spent some time getting to know Max and chatting with my client about her recent challenges trying to get him adjusted to her home while managing his medical issues. Within minutes, Max responded to my clicker and began pushing me to click more. At the end of the session, he tried to engage me in hopes of earning a cookie. I asked him for a "Sit," and he stared at me blankly. I knew Max could sit because he'd been doing it consistently on cue during our time together.

When Max didn't respond, I let it go. I said, "Okay," and turned to walk away. I gave him a choice on whether to interact with me or not. As I took my first step in the opposite direction, I heard Max's nails scrambling on the hardwood floor beneath him. Before my second step touched the floor, he whooshed by me, turned around, and sat perfectly in front of me, with the poise of a marble statue. I responded with praises and ear scratches. When I tried to leave once more, Max leaped up. I asked for a "Sit" again, and this time he couldn't bring his bottom to the ground fast enough.

Max reminds us that everybody likes to have choices in their world. Why should dogs like yours and mine be any different?

To put it simply, give the dog a choice whenever possible and honor your dog's vote. Making choices should come before task-based training because it sets the stage for higher learning. By allowing your dog to have some control over their own life, you create an environment for them to grow in confidence and develop a more peaceful co-existence with dogs and humans.

Confident by Choice is all about challenging conventional approaches, considering your dog's perspective, encouraging creativity, and transforming their relationship with themselves as well as their relationship with their #1: you.

There's no one-size-fits-all recipe because many variables shape a dog's personality, including genetics, formative early experiences, health, and environment.

Confident by Choice introduces you and your dog to many strategies and tactics (let's call them "spices"). Think of it like your famous stew recipe. You start with a classic recipe, then season to taste. Once you learn how to read your dog, you'll see what's working and what's not and adjust your "training recipe" accordingly. While you may up the paprika and pull back on the cumin, your friend and her pup go heavy on the cayenne. But if your results taste good to you and your dog, you've got a recipe to lean on for life.

Photo courtesy of Unsplash - Merve Sehirli

Chapter 2

The Dogma of Confident by Choice

Vote early, vote often, and respect the vote cast.

Whether you got your dog as a puppy or adopted an older dog with a long history, it's never too late to start incorporating the *Confident by Choice* approach. You can make so many changes to your everyday interactions with your dog that can have a huge impact with minimal time commitment from you. Consider all the opportunities on any given day where you can incorporate this different way of interacting with your dog.

Let's look at the Montessori School and its unique approach to educating children. The more I learned about their approach to teaching children, the more I realized how it applied to my approach to working with dogs. The American Montessori Society sums up their methods in the following way: "Given the freedom and support to question, probe deeply, and make connections, Montessori students grow up to be confident, enthusiastic, and self-directed learners and citizens, accountable to both themselves and their community. They think critically, work collaboratively, and act boldly and with integrity." Some of their basic teachings can also apply to dogs if we just replace human references with dog references. Each child is valued as a unique individual, and students enjoy freedom within limits while being supported to become active seekers of knowledge.

There are five components of the Montessori Education system, and two of them, when applied to your dog, can make a big difference in their behavior: child-directed work and uninterrupted work periods.

In child-directed work, students are given agency to self-select work, leading to intrinsic motivation and sustained attention. Why? Because they chose what they wanted to do at that particular time. Most dogs enjoy that same sense of empowerment.

Montessori also provides uninterrupted work periods, which they describe as "extended periods of free choice," so students can work at their own pace and without interruption. This allows children to learn to enjoy the journey and not race to the result. Both of these components are part of the *Confidence by Choice* method.

Consider prison life. Many inmates have schedules planned out for them with little to no opportunity to make choices. But incredible outcomes become possible when choices and opportunities are presented to them through educational and career-focused programs. According to the US Department of Justice, inmates who participate in correctional education programs are 43% less likely to end up back in prison than those who don't, while inmates who worked in prison industries were 24% less likely to return to prison and 14% more likely to gain employment after release.

Like the environments that keep both children and adults from achieving their potential, most dogs live scripted lives with few opportunities to make choices. Humans decide what their dog eats, when they eat, when they go for a walk, where they go for a walk, when they should get up in the morning, and when they should go to bed.

But what if your dog is so overwhelmed that they're incapable of making a choice, or the concept is so foreign to them that they don't know how to indicate their preference?

Present two options.
If your dog so much as flicks their eyes towards one or the other, praise them for making a stellar choice and let them move forward.

Go at their pace.
In severely shut-down dogs or dogs with no history of being given a chance to vote, choice can be a foreign concept. Give them time to gain confidence and understand the "game." They'll begin to choose one option you present over another. Over time, that same once-despondent or perplexed dog will change and give a very clear, happy signal about what they want the moment you ask.

Try this:
In the evening, let your dog choose between two snacks. Ask them to sit and place their choices on the floor. If they instantly know what they want, they'll pounce on it. If they investigate both options before deciding, they might paw at the one they want or lay in front of it. This is a dog who appreciates being given a choice and isn't afraid to clearly indicate his preference.

Confident by Choice™

Neighborhood Negotiations: A Lesson from Diesel

Diesel thrives on structure. He needs to know what's going on and what's expected of him to feel secure. Giving him these three small choices in his everyday life has helped to bolster his confidence:

Choosing his cookies.
Before each walk, I lay down two to three bags of cookies and ask him to pick one. After sniffing each of them, he lies down in front of the one he wants so that his chosen bag of cookies sits between his front paws.

Choosing his walks.
Diesel's walks offer a lot of options. When we get out of the car, he decides which direction we go. At cross streets, he can choose his path to determine the length of the walk. When he's tired or the temperature's hot, he'll choose a shorter route.

Negotiating the length of the walk.
Sometimes I'm not up for a long walk. If Diesel wants to take another route, I stop and ask him if he's sure he doesn't want to take the shorter path.

Sometimes he'll let me know that he really, really wants to go the other way. If time allows, I'll appease him and go the way he wants. But more times than not, he'll appease me and choose the path I asked him to consider.

Cultivating a relationship of compromise with your dog builds trust and respect. When you give them the opportunity to vote often and respect their vote, you'll see that they begin to see and respect your vote when you really need them to.

Chapter 3

Infuse Choice in Surprises

*Turn your dog's unfavorable reactions
into a simple matter of choice.*

Many dogs will startle at the sudden onset of a sound or sight. Some dogs
will recover quickly, but for others, that loud bang or cat-sighting can
ruin their whole day. There's a term for these surprises in the dog training
world: SEC, or Sudden Environmental Changes.

For example, a familiar stroll down a neighborhood street could be interrupted by a blaring air horn that startles you both. Or, you turn a corner
in the hallway of your apartment building, and a large, strange dog is
barreling toward you and your dog.

Chances are, you're thinking of an SEC moment you've had with your
dog right now. Fortunately, there are a number of ways to take the startle
out of SECs.

Talk about it.
Acknowledge startling events to your dog by having a conversation about
them. For example, if a car suddenly backfires, you can turn to your dog
and exclaim, "HOLY COW! That was LOUD! I heard that, too, and that
scared the daylights out of me." Whenever I do this with a dog, their
body language relaxes. If a cloud bubble appeared over their head, I
imagine it would say something like, "Thank goodness you heard it, too.
I thought I was imagining things!"

Can We Talk?: A Lesson from Iris

Confined to a tiny, controlled world for her first few years, Iris didn't have the opportunity to experience new things. While she has confidence in her daily routine, any change or surprise causes her to become highly suspicious, fearful and shut down. While working with Iris and her mom, we discovered that engaging her in conversations about things that concern her instantly calms her suspicions and fears.

Chattering about foreign objects, strange circumstances, or sudden surprises gives your dog the impression that the potentially scary things aren't a big deal. And because predictability is key to dogs like Iris, you can name and acknowledge the people, things, and happenings around you to help them feel familiar to your dog. Because if you say it's okay, your dog will eventually believe you.

Photo courtesy of Unsplash - Jenny Marvin

Give a heads up.

If you know something is about to change, you can warn your dog. Let's say you're about to walk past a house with a dog who typically snarls at your dog from behind his fence.

Tell your dog that Fido is barking because he's jealous that he's stuck behind the fence: "Boy, I bet he'd love to be out here with us smelling all of these great smells and getting lots of exercise." The more you normalize this event by giving a quick head's up and talking in an upbeat voice, the less anxious your dog will be.

Tricks and Treats: A Lesson from Nash

Nash, a large Lab mix, was terrified of loud, unexpected noises. While working with Nash and his family, a car suddenly backfired. Nash instantly froze and planted himself on the ground, so his humans started pulling on his leash.

I interrupted their well-intended efforts and asked them to stop, stand near Nash, and acknowledge the scary noise. I showed them what I meant by talking to Nash in an exaggerated voice, telling him that I heard the backfire.

He wouldn't settle down, so I sat beside him and continued talking, just like telling a child a bedtime story. After a few minutes, I felt him relax under my hand, so I stood up and asked him if he wanted to join me. As we made our way back to the car, I let Nash sniff in the grass and let him decide what direction we were going.

We stopped at a short stone wall, and I showed the family to ask Nash to put his front paws up on the wall. They gave him cookies when he stretched tall. We then asked him to jump onto the wall and walk to the end. Next, we asked him for a "Sit" and gave him a cookie. Quite pleased with himself, Nash gained a spring in his step that hadn't been there since the car backfired.

Giving your dog easy activities and chances to earn cookies can take their mind away from startling events that cause them to shut down. Next time an SEC threatens to steal your dog's joy, tell a story, introduce opportunities for fun and cookies, and bring back the happy dog you know and love.

  Confident by Choice™

Play the name game.
Naming things provides familiarity. Imagine you go to a party where the only person you know is the person that invited you. Making small talk with strangers is intimidating. That is, until the host starts pointing out people and telling you their names and a little something about them so you can strike up a conversation. Suddenly you feel more comfortable, and engaging those strangers doesn't feel scary. Get where I'm going? Your dog feels the same way!

Name It and Claim It: A Lesson from Diesel

Multiple times a day, my dog Diesel barked furiously at the window when he would see two small brown dogs walk up and down our street. He was excited, wanted information, and expressed a whole mix of feelings that he couldn't process.

Whenever we saw them, I told my dog the "brown puppies" are out for their walk and fed him multiple cookies. After ten times of doing this at the sight of those dogs, my dog now recognizes the phrase "brown puppies," and his overarousal turns into excitement at the opportunity to earn more cookies.

Photo by M. Nicole Fischer Photography

Chapter 4

Let Your Pup Set the Pace

It's their journey, after all.

If you don't have the time to work at the dog's pace, wait to initiate an activity or outing until you have the time to support them and accommodate their speed or lack thereof. In the same way, if you find yourself becoming impatient with your dog, immediately abandon the activity.

I've spent massive amounts of time waiting for the dog to tell me what the next move should be. If something scary happens and the dog wants to freeze, I'll take a seat on the grass and let the dog decide when we move on. If we come up to a slatted footbridge and the dog balks at it, I ask them if they can do it. If they say, "No," we go the other way and try again another day. I don't mind the wait because I know that with every choice I give them, they're gaining confidence, and, one day, they'll trot out in front of me and confidently walk across like it was no big deal.

In short: your dog will "figure it out" on their own timeline, even if that means that they trust that when they say "No, I can't do this," you'll honor that request and adjust accordingly. There are proven training methods that can help dogs to overcome their fears that involve minimal exposure to the scary thing and methods that train them to perform a different behavior in the presence of the scary thing. Still, these are task-driven training methods, and some dogs aren't in the mental space to learn them just yet. Those methods have their place in the world, but if you start giving your dog choices early on in your relationship, the dog develops confidence, and there will be fewer scary things to worry about because the dog will be able to work through them on their own.

Along your journey, you'll receive plenty of unsolicited advice from people who will criticize your methods: "Who's in charge of that walk?" or "Just pull the leash. They'll get up and follow you." Rather than pivot to traditional methods that cause your dog stress, you can rest assured that you're supporting your dog's wellness, building their confidence, and growing trust in your relationship.

The truth is that dogs have good and bad days like us. Every day comes with new challenges, so we need to read their emotions and adjust our plans on the fly, just like we do for ourselves and others we love.

Photo courtesy of Unsplash - Marcus Wallis

From Driveway Pancake to Prancing in the Park:
A Lesson from Louis

A lifelong homebody, Louis' fears kicked in whenever he was outdoors. To help Louis with his goal of comfortably venturing outside, I enlisted my pup to join us on a walk. We made it to the top of the driveway, and then Louis flattened like a pancake on the ground. I asked Louis if he was sure he didn't want to join us on the walk, and he didn't even flinch. So, I met Louis where he was and sat on the grass next to him. Eventually, Louis got up and walked another 20 feet only to pancake again.

We tried again the next day with similar results. Although this time, Louis didn't stop at the top of my driveway. He walked to the house next door before he pancaked. The following day, Louis walked with my dog and me past three houses and then froze - but he didn't pancake. I asked him if he had enough, and Louis immediately turned and dragged us back to the house. At that moment, I gave Louis a vote and respected his choice.

By the end of the first week, Louis was jauntily strolling up the street before turning around and coming back home.

When the next weekend rolled around, Louis hopped into my SUV so he, my dog, and I could drive to a nearby park. The three of us enjoyed a lovely 30-minute walk, and any time Louis got nervous, we stopped and waited it out. Each time, he chose to continue our walk together over heading back to the truck.

Photo courtesy of Unsplash - Fotografu

Sharing space does more than you think.
Simply sharing space with a dog who isn't yet ready to express a choice lets your dog know that you're both physically and emotionally "there" for them.

But what does it mean to "share space"?
Sharing space is exactly as it sounds. Just sit in the same area as your dog, sharing space with them. Let your dog dictate how close or how far you sit by them. Allow them to scootch away if they like.

Patience is the biggest obstacle for us humans in these circumstances. But instead of dismissing their need for downtime, use this opportunity for downtime of your own. You can meditate, listen to music, read a book, scroll through social media, or play a game on your mobile device with the sound muted, so your dog has the opportunity to take in the sounds of the environment.

Flexing the Statue: A Lesson from Andy

A downtrodden foster dog, Andy was completely shut down. He refused to move, go outside to potty, or even look at the people and dogs in his foster home. Instead, he kept his face and body pointed towards the wall.

When I met Andy, he didn't turn around to see me or even twitch an ear when I tried to sweet-talk him from a distance. One of the rules I live by when it comes to dogs is to meet the dog where he is mentally and emotionally, so I observed him from a distance for a while until I determined that he wasn't a threat to me. I walked over to his dog bed, sat on its edge with my back facing his back, and sat there for an hour chatting with my friend.

After a while, my friend and I moved into the kitchen. I sat on the floor with my dog on my lap while my friend prepared some tea. Suddenly, I looked up to find Andy walking cautiously into the kitchen. He sniffed my hair and sat behind me, facing my back and sneaking peeks over my shoulder at the other person and dogs in the room. Neither of us humans reacted.

When the tea was finished, we went back to the living room, and I sat on Andy's dog bed again. This time, he decided to join me. Eventually, I pet him with the back of my hand ever so lightly. Within an hour, he rested his head under my hand for more petting.

The true test was whether he would go outside to potty on his own. I got up, walked to the door, and gently invited him outside with us. Much to our astonishment, Andy walked out of his own free will.

When you meet your dog where they are on their own terms, you give them a choice. That builds the kind of trust that empowers your dog to move forward in their own time, assured you're there for them no matter what happens.

Confident by Choice™

Manage change with empathy.
Life happens, and we do our best with the hand we are dealt. Sometimes dogs need to be rehomed. That doesn't mean that they aren't loved. It means that life doesn't always go how we want it to. I used to think a dog's history would guide my work with the dog, but I no longer find this true.

It doesn't matter where a dog comes from. You can't change the past, but you can guide your dog on a different path. Help them move towards a brighter future by using the *Confident by Choice* approach, meeting them where they are, and defining your leadership role in the relationship by your kindness and understanding.

Photo courtesy of Unsplash - Cynthia Smith

Chapter 5

Value the Little Things

*Keeping your dog's world small
helps them grow.*

Sometimes you'll meet a dog who isn't capable of making a
choice … yet.

For those souls with no prior experience walking up steps, hearing the
sounds on TV, or getting a whiff of dinner cooking, keeping their world
small is your best bet. Think about it this way: If you landed on Mercury
and were suddenly surrounded by strange creatures who spoke a different
language and moved bizarrely, wouldn't you be overwhelmed? Some
dogs see the human world in the same way.

If you share a life with a dog who behaves this way, understand that
they're not well-versed in voting. Begin with them by slowly removing
choices and introducing new experiences to help them acclimate and
feel safe.

As the dog gets more comfortable with the routine you've created,
you'll start to see a spark of curiosity. Soon enough, your dog will tell
you they're ready to make some small choices. Once you reach this
transformative step, ask your dog to decide on the following:

- Would they like to go for a walk or stay home?
- Would they like to eat in their crate or in the corner?
- Would they like to relax on the couch with you or lounge
  on the floor?

There's no wrong answer when you give your dog these types of votes because you've chosen safe scenarios that let your dog be successful no matter what they decide.

Small Steps Gain Ground, Too: A Lesson from Conor

Conor was a foster dog who was terrified of the world. He only wanted to be in the backyard, huddled under a shed. He was a nervous wreck in the house and refused to come out of his crate in the bedroom.

After two days of working with Conor, I took him out of the crate and shut the door behind him. He found the farthest corner of the bedroom and hunkered down there.

Two days later, I led him out of the bedroom and shut the bedroom door behind him. He slowly made his way out to the living area and lay in the crate in the living room. One day, I closed that crate door when we went for a walk, so Conor had to find a different spot to hang out when he came back home. Each time we blocked access. After about two weeks of slowly making his world larger, he began hanging out with me on his own, and we no longer needed to block his access to his safe places. Soon enough, that comfort transferred to his hiding spot under the shed.

As his confidence grew, Conor continued to visit the man cave under the shed, but he'd happily come out when called because he knew he was being invited to play, go on a walk, or enjoy dinner. By gradually expanding your dog's small world to a larger yet familiar one, they'll explore in comfort - just like Conor.

Chapter 6

Respect the Struggle Bus

*Sometimes our less-than-stellar choices
are just a matter of our circumstances.*

Our human world and dog world have clear differences. We communicate verbally while dogs look to body language to read one another. While humans use body language as a secondary indicator, another dog or human's stance is their #1 source of information. That's why the "bad decisions" we see our dogs make are pretty logical to them.

Imagine if you visited a foreign country without knowing their customs. You were invited to a dinner, given a time you didn't understand, and showed up in jeans 30 minutes late. How would you feel if you walked in and everyone was dressed in formal wear, already enjoying the first course? Your first feeling may be embarrassment, but at some point you may experience anger because nobody told you what was expected of you. This is what our dogs go through every time we don't communicate our expectations for them.

Keep a lookout.
To support your dog in the event of a struggle-bus moment or full-blown meltdown, it's important to know what your dog looks like when they start to get uncomfortable, along with places and events that cause them to stress or act out. Once you identify your dog's stress ticks, you can better manage sticky situations and protect them from total exposure to what scares them.

 Confident by Choice™

For example, do loud construction vehicles cause your dog to pin back their ears just before losing control? Start with the obvious and don't walk on known routes where those trucks travel. If you see one coming, turn at the nearest cross street or stand behind a vehicle parked on the road to gain distance from them, so their roar sounds softer.

Be mindful of your dog's trigger state.

Isn't a spider easier to handle when it's across the room rather than crawling on your arm? When your dog is close to a trigger, their body can engage in a fight or flight response that prevents them from hearing you or seeing anything but the trigger. They aren't willfully ignoring you. They've involuntarily tuned everything out to hyper-focus on the scary or threatening thing.

Never put your hand in front of your dog's face when in that state because you may startle them even further and provoke a bite. It's like if you're watching a scary movie and someone touches your shoulder and spooks you, causing you to launch your bowl of popcorn across the room.

Employ distraction tactics to ease their reaction.

The farther you can get from the trigger, the better you'll be able to work with your dog to overcome the situation. Unfortunately, sometimes you can't move your dog away from the trigger.

In this instance, you can:

Tap them on the hind end.

Once you do this, be sure to remove your hand quickly. Sometimes a tactile tap is enough to move your dog's attention away from the trigger and back to you.

Wave food near your dog's nose.

Approach from the front so your dog can see it's coming. Be careful not to forcefully shove the food into your dog's face, remembering the previous advice about getting too close to the biting end of the dog when your dog is deep in fight-or-flight mode.

Drop food or a beloved toy in front of them.

Start from a few inches in front of their face or above their head. Sometimes the falling motion is enough to break their focus so you can move them away from the trigger.

Avoid face-to-face interactions.
Getting into a staring contest with your dog probably won't end well, especially when they're in a tough situation.

Have some distance? Give them a vote.
If there's enough distance between your dog and the threat, let them take in the information available and allow your dog to decide if they want to take it to the next level or shrug it off. When your dog determines if something is a threat or not, their body language shows alertness – still stance, upright position, pointed ears that may rotate to take in sounds, and eyes focused like laser beams. If you know they're headed toward a meltdown, use the tips in this chapter to help them calm down.

Plan an escape route.
With good sightlines, you can veer off your walking path and continue with an enjoyable stroll. A lot of paths have bump-out loops and intersections that support a quick pivot for you and your dog. If needed, cut across the grass because, in the end, gaining distance from threats is key to your dog's comfort.

Photo by Sanja Popovic - Models Kelly and Zoe

Keep on moving.
Standing still in the face of potential danger isn't a good survival technique, and this well-meaning reaction on your part can cause your dog to make poor decisions. Movement helps your dog maintain control because it keeps them preoccupied and gives them an outlet for all the energy inside them.

Photo by Sanja Popovic - Models Kelly and Bear

Move to greener pastures with hand bops.
If your dog is amped up and trotting in a different direction won't calm them down, teach your dog to touch their nose to your hand, or as I like to call them, "hand bops." Engaging in hand bops while walking away from the trigger can benefit your dog's mental state. Follow the steps below to teach your pup this stress-taming exercise. Note: You'll need a clicker during training.

Step 1. Present and hold your hand close to your dog's nose, about one to three inches away. Click when your dog moves toward or looks at your hand. Don't click near your dog's ears as it may frighten them or hurt their ears. Remove your target hand after each click and give them a treat. Repeat multiple times. Removing your target hand after each repetition helps to initiate interest from your dog.

If your dog goes right ahead and bumps or touches his nose on the palm of your hand, fantastic! Click as their nose hits your hand, then remove it and give them the treat.

Repeat Step 1 multiple times until your dog consistently touches his nose to your hand when it's presented up close.

Step 2. Move your target hand in various positions about 1-3 inches away from the dog's nose. Try left, right, slightly higher, and a little lower. If you can see your dog is purposely touching his nose to your hand when it's presented in any direction, you're ready to add the cue.

Step 3. Verbally say your cue "Touch", and then present your hand. Separating the verbal from your hand presentation by just a second will help them process that the word "touch" is associated with bopping the hand. Click as their nose hits your hand. Remove your hand, treat, and repeat.

Step 4. Hold your hand further away from your dog so they have to take a few more steps to follow or get to the target. As they come towards your hand target, begin to move it away, so they follow and click to acknowledge any move they make toward the target. They only need to take a couple of steps at first and don't need to touch the hand target. Reward efforts with immediate clicks and treats.

Step 5. Move around in different directions, having your dog follow your target hand. Limit your steps at first, and gradually increase the number of steps you take before you click, then treat your dog.

Be sure to practice with your opposite hand as well so your dog learns that hand-targeting applies to each hand.

Let's play!
Once your dog understands that the presentation of either of your hands means they should touch their nose to the target hand, you can turn this exercise into a fast and fun game. This is the perfect game to play when you need to get your dog's attention.

With your dog in front of you, present your hand and say "Touch" in a playful tone. When they touch it, raise your other hand in another position and say, "Touch." Give them a cookie.

   Confident by Choice™

Repeat these steps multiple times with your hands in different positions. Give cookies at random times, so your dog is still being rewarded for the hand touches, but the order of rewards hasn't formed a pattern.

Hold your hand high to get jumping touches, hold it low behind and between your legs for your dog to go between your legs, hold it out to the side on your left, and then pop the other hand out to the side on the right. Now you're playing "Whack a Mole," and soon enough, the chase outshines the need for cookies because the game becomes a reward.

What if your dog won't move towards your presented target hand? Take your hand away behind your back. Present it again a little closer or farther away from the previous unsuccessful attempt.

Try rubbing that target palm in aromatic food to capture their interest or secure a piece of food in your target hand by folding your thumb inward. Click as their nose gets close, remove the target hand, and give them a cookie.

If they're still not getting it:

- Consider using a different hand position. Sometimes a dog can have negative feelings towards an open palm, or they've been trained that a palm means something else. If this is the case, try holding out two fingers for them to bop with their nose.

- You may be holding your target hand too high.

- If your dog is using you for balance, try extending your arm so the target hand isn't as close to your body. That way, your dog will have nothing to put their paws on.

Photo by Susan Hinson - Models Bader and Sonia

Keep their eyes on the prize with the Find It game.
When you're walking in close quarters or have lots of curves on your path, you may not know someone is coming at you until they suddenly appear. It isn't always possible to duck out of the way, so lean on this "Find It" game that you can play either in place or while moving.

Step 1. Start in a quiet environment and sit by your dog, either on a low stool or the ground, and keep food in your hand behind your back. You want the food to be easily accessible, but not in front of their face in a way that distracts them.

Step 2. Say, "Find it," and drop a piece of food on the ground close to your dog. It's imperative to separate the verbal cue of "Find it" from the food drop. This gives your dog a split second to process the cue you just gave.

Step 3. Count ten treats and repeat the steps above. Give your dog a break while you reload your treat hand.

Step 4. Next, start a new session. This time, when you say, "Find it", pause a split second more before you drop the food. See if your dog looks to the ground for the cookies because that's where the treats appeared.

   Confident by Choice™

If they look at the ground when you say, "Find it" and not at you or your hand, give them multiple cookies in rapid-fire succession to make this response memorable.

Step 5. When your dog reliably looks at the ground when you say "find it", raise your body, so you're no longer sitting on the ground. Go for a short stool or rest on your knees. This adds a little height to the drop, so your dog has to make a more conscious decision to look at the ground. Next, go from that position to sitting in a regular chair. For your final position, you'll stand up straight and drop the cookies in front of your dog.

You can use the Find It game as you walk down the street and dogs charge at fences, barking while you pass.

Loudly say, "Find it," and your dog will be elated to play their favorite game as the neighbor dogs aggressively bark behind the fence alongside you. When your dog looks at you or the ground, toss a cookie as though you're bowling so it lands a foot or two in front of them. Now they have to scurry ahead to get it. As soon as your dog swallows the treat, say, "Find it" again and bowl another.

If you're in the thick of a situation, don't bowl the cookies too far because the farther your dog gets from you, the more you lose connection and the more likely they'll lunge at the dogs behind the fence.

Once you get your timing down and your dog understands what "Find it" means, this game keeps them engaged and entertained while you're on the move, no matter what your surroundings may be.

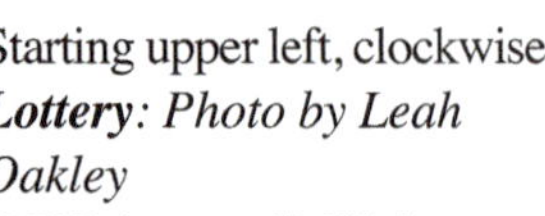
Starting upper left, clockwise:
Lottery: Photo by Leah Oakley
CGH Asgaard's Welcome to the New Age: Photo by Martha McCormick
Kagan: Photo by Susan Hinson
Frankee: Photo by Sue Iobst
Cody: Photo by Siny Tsang

Inspire Confidence with the Superhero Stand.
The Superhero Stand distracts your dog from an oncoming scary thing by giving them a task and rewarding them with treats.

I dubbed this position the "Superhero Stand" because it reminded me of how a superhero poses with their feet planted firmly, chest out, and chin up. They always punctuate this stance with a confident gaze - just like dogs do.

Step 1. The Superhero Stand happens when your dog puts two front paws on an elevated surface such as a step or a curb. It works best if the surface is not higher than the dog's elbow. First, find the sweet spot for your dog's height and emotional comfort.

Look for something that only has one elevated surface such as a curb, platform, or stool.

Walk your dog over to the platform and lure them up with a cookie, so their front paws rest on the platform. As soon as their front feet are on it, acknowledge their achievement by clicking with a clicker or saying "Yes" if you aren't using a clicker.

Once you've marked the behavior, deliver a cookie to your dog's mouth while their front feet are still on the platform.

Confident by Choice™

Step 2. Toss a cookie behind your dog so they have to run away from the platform to retrieve it (this is also known as a "cookie reset").

Step 3. Encourage your dog to put their front paws on the platform again and repeat the previous steps: Mark the behavior, deliver the cookie to their mouth, and toss a reset cookie. After a few reps, stop luring your dog back to the platform with food and wait to see if they put their front paws on the platform without any prompting.

Make sure you're looking at the platform and not looking your dog in the eye. Looking at the platform conveys that what you want concerns the platform.

Once your dog begins to reliably place their front paws on the platform, you can then name the behavior. You'll want to say it before they put their feet up.

Step 4. Now you can ask for the Superhero Stand on different objects. You want to build value in the behavior, so your dog doesn't have to think twice about doing it when asked because they know a cookie will come their way.

If you're out and your dog suddenly startles, take full advantage of anything in your sight. It could be a curb, a bench, or a log.

You can also train your dog to put their front feet on you:

- Lift your knee so your thigh is parallel to the ground and your shin is perpendicular to the ground. That way, your dog can put their feet on top of your raised foot. Tough to balance? Try the following options.

- Place one foot in front of you and flex your foot so your heel is on the ground and your toes point up. Train your dog to put his paws onto the ends of your toes. Since your flexed toes provide much less surface area for your dog, practice this one at home until your dog has perfected it.

- Go down on one knee with your other knee bent in front of you. Ask your dog to put his paws up on your thigh parallel to the ground. Be wary that this might be painful if you're on a rough surface.

Chapter 7

Check Yourself

Claiming your role in your dog's growth journey means you have choices to make, too.

No matter your experience with dogs, you can make simple life changes that can significantly impact your dog. There's always room to build a deeper bond with your four-legged friend, from the first step in your training journey to the steps far down your path.

Know their moves.
While dogs have a spoken language complete with barks, growls, yips, and howls, they don't have the verbal language humans do. Sure, you can teach them words and make associations, but they'll never say "Hello" in response to you waving to them. But when you return home after work, your dog greets you by jumping, wagging, barking, rubbing against you, and rejoicing that you're back home. While they didn't belt out an enthusiastic "Hello!" they said it in their own canine way.

Translating your dog's body language and reactions can help you communicate with them more effectively. Mind these signs that your dog is feeling uncomfortable:
- Ears pinned back
- Lip licking
- Yawning
- Looking away
- Tail tucked
- Low growl
- Whale eyes (the whites of their eyes display)
- Avoidance of the object or area

Photo courtesy of Unsplash - Michelle Tresemer

- Freeze (dog doesn't move)
- Displacement behaviors like sniffing the ground, acting inappropriately cute or silly, or scratching or grooming their own bodies

This is not an exhaustive list, but it's a good start to knowing when your best friend needs your support. Want to learn more? There are some excellent books on canine body language in the Resources section.

See things from your dog's point of view.
Often, we humans aren't very clear when dealing with other humans who speak the same language. Imagine how unclear things get when we try to communicate with our dogs, who lean on body language to convey their feelings.

Consider this: When a dog has been taught that "Down" means to lay down flat on the ground, they usually learn this stance by starting from a sit and then moving into the down position.

Dogs don't usually learn to lay down from a standing position but think about how many times you've seen a dog jump up at a person on their hind legs, and their human tells them "Down!" The dog has no idea how to respond because, in their mind, a "Down" only happens from a sitting position. In the dog's experience, "Down" uses a whole different set of muscles.

Now, the human doesn't care if the dog lays flat on the ground. They just want the dog to not jump on the other human. But see how their message gets lost in translation?

Instead of "Down," use an "Off" cue: Don't touch the thing you're standing or jumping on. I teach "Off" when the dog balances his hind legs so he understands that "Off" means planting all four paws on the ground.

Since dogs understand body language better than verbal cues, make sure your body communicates what you want your dog to know. There is a hierarchy in body language, and eye contact is a powerful indicator for your dog. Usually, when you make direct eye contact with a dog, they stop what they are doing and look at you. If you want a dog to look at something, look them in the eye and then deliberately look at something else. Most of the time, the dog will follow your gaze.

Patience is a virtue (and a necessity).
Dogs that lack confidence or who haven't been taught how to "learn" require a lot of patience. They don't do things on typical timelines or have the reactions humans expect them to. It's up to us to help change their responses. I say "genuine patience" because dogs aren't fooled by humans easily. If you're letting your dog work through an issue while tapping your foot or looking all around the room, that's not patience. Sure, you're waiting it out, but your body language tells your dog you're not on board with the process. These unconscious actions interfere with your dog's ability to focus on working through the issue at hand.

If you don't have time to work at your dog's pace, work through the issue later. For example, if you have an appointment and need to leave the house in 30 minutes, training your dog to walk around the block is best saved until later.

Be their biggest fan, even if that means quiet encouragement.
Celebrate the small successes to let your dog know just how awesome they are.

Use a very kind tone, but avoid taking on an over-the-top speech pattern. Erupting into a full-blown victory cheer can inadvertently startle your dog. Some dogs can't even handle a passing comment like, "You're a rockstar!" For those dogs, simply say, "Okay, we're walking again." Or say nothing at all.

                                    Confident by Choice™

If you walk two steps and your dog pancakes, make sure your body language doesn't express frustration or impatience. Your attitude should convey a gentle acceptance, "Okay, now we are sitting in the grass." Treat each movement matter-of-factly and try not to add any emotion.

It's a joyous occasion when a dog with big feelings makes it through a whole group class without a barking or lunging scene. Or that dog can work through all the exercises just like every other dog in the class. If a dog is struggling mentally or emotionally, success may be simply walking into the training facility and hanging out for five minutes before having to leave. Instead of taking these victories for granted, join your dog in celebrating them. This gives them the confidence to continue their progress and feel good while doing it.

Photo courtesy of Unsplash - Joseph Pearson

Chapter 8

Deal with the Bumps in the Road

Mistakes happen, but there's no need to dwell on them. That goes for you and your dog.

Don't get bogged down in "paralysis by analysis." Overanalyzing where things went off the rails can stall your dog's growth journey. Of course, it's okay to hit the pause button and regroup, but don't let too much time pass before you try different solutions. The longer you wait and fret about the issue, the less confidence you and your dog will have in dealing with future setbacks. There's no evidence that dogs dwell on things the way we humans do, so cut yourself some slack and move on because your dog probably already has.

Think of a toddler who trips and falls on the grass. The toddler looks to their parents for a cue to laugh or cry. If the adult rushes in and makes a fuss over the child, there's a good chance the toddler will erupt in tears. If the adult laughs it off and turns it into a funny event, the child will end up laughing also. Dogs pick up on your reactions in the very same way.

In another example, a dog and their handler were in a sporting competition, and the handler made a mistake and cost them a qualifying score. The handler dropped their shoulders and let out a loud sigh, and the dog immediately shut down even though the handler wasn't frustrated with the dog at all. They were upset about their own performance, not the dog's. The problem is that the dog can't decipher this. The dog just senses disappointment.

When my dog and I don't qualify at sporting events, I celebrate anyway. My dog doesn't need to know we didn't "win." He's playing a game for me, so my dog is always right as far as I'm concerned. This may seem strange, but when you build a relationship with your dog based on trust, you quickly learn how celebrating small things can make the biggest difference.

Know when to fold 'em.
In the words of the famous Kenny Rogers song, *"Know when to hold 'em. Know when to fold 'em. Know when to walk away and know when to run."* Some things just aren't worth pursuing for various reasons:

- The dog doesn't have the tools to cope
- The human doesn't have the tools to cope
- The human can't control other people's or dogs' behavior
- The human doesn't have access to escape hatches

Scrapping a plan doesn't make you a quitter. It makes you a kind human being who considers your dog's capacity to handle the situation. If you paid for a class and your dog is struggling, it's okay to put them in the car with food or a stuffed toy. Go back into the class by yourself so you can take that lesson home. That way, you can work with your dog in a more comfortable environment.

Chapter 9

Own Your Dog's Story

Ditch expectations and focus on what's possible.

Many people say, "Nope, my dog won't do that," and then they're blown away when their dog does precisely that. Psychology tells us that approaching a task with a negative attitude will influence the outcome (and not in a good way). Don't assume the dog won't do something because they can surprise you.

This doesn't mean you should proactively choose activities that will push your dog beyond their comfort zone. But if you're in a position to ask your dog to do something that won't impact their mental state, give it a shot and see what happens.

Temper your reaction.
This scenario occasionally happens in group classes: The instructor explains an exercise, and the human handler immediately says that their dog won't perform simple gestures like nose bops. The human handler tries it, and their dog touches their hand, astounding them.

This can go one of two ways: The human's excitement can encourage their dog to repeat the action, or their dog will shut down. It pays to have neutral reactions until you know how your dog will react. Once you know the praise your pup prefers, repeat it every time they surprise you.

Your dog's journey is as unique as they are.
The ideas in this book aren't "training" but rather a philosophy on working with dogs. Training is a formula that everyone can apply. For example, clicker training is black and white. The clicker marks the dog's behavior, and a reward acknowledges that the dog did something you wanted.

When working with dogs, the world becomes many shades of gray. Your approach must be subjective, fluid, and ready to adjust on the fly as variables change and as your dog's needs change along with them. Dogs aren't robots. They're affected by many of the same things that humans are. When you're working with a sensitive dog, you need to be observant and translate their responses and your immediate environment into an operational plan that can flex at a moment's notice.

When you know what makes your dog uncomfortable, you can plan. On the flip side, when you know what makes your dog comfortable, you can leverage those things to your benefit. Remember that just because something works once doesn't mean it will work every time, so build up your toolbox so you have various tools to choose from.

We all have bad days.
Your dog may snuggle up to a man with a beard one day but the next day react poorly to that man because they have an upset stomach. This has nothing to do with the man, and if you're keeping tabs on your dog's physical and emotional state, you'll know that. We can all become irritable when we don't feel good, so let's extend our dogs the same amount of grace we want others to give us in our off moments.

Chapter 10

Discover What Makes Your Dog Tick

The trusty clicker, the fuzzy orange ball: every dog has their favorite. What's your dog's security blanket?

The more you learn what makes your dog tick, the better solutions you'll find. There's no one-size-fits-all option, so think creatively to dream up tactics, toys, and treats that will support the dog in front of you. Don't be afraid to get a little wacky.

For example, if you know your dog loves a ball, bring it with you on walks. When you see something potentially scary, bounce the ball in front of your dog. They may surprise you by snatching it out of the air and completely breezing by what could have been an unsettling distraction.

Find Their Favorites in Unexpected Places:
A Lesson from Diesel

My dog wasn't a fan of toys when we were training for a sporting competition. The instructors wanted him to play tug or run toward a toy stuffed with food. None of those things interested Diesel until we were in a group class in a horse arena, and he left me. He had never left my side in a class before.

When I figured out where he went, I saw his front paws resting on a large plastic bucket and his head burrowed deep in its contents. The arena owner told me the bucket contained dirty wool from sheep they had recently sheared. Seeing the response it elicited in my dog, I promptly asked the owner if I could take a bag of it home. I brought the wool home, stuffed it into a thick tube sock, and tied a knot on the open end to close the sock. Suddenly, my dog was tugging with me so enthusiastically as he had never done before. He continued retrieving the stuffed sock so that we could tug some more.

I took the "sheep sock" on the road with us. When we came across something worrisome to my dog, I tossed the sock away from the scary thing and ran toward it with my dog. We reached the sock at the same time and added tug into the mix.

This sock helped us through scary incidents many, many times. And, of course, I continued to collect tossed fleece from the arena to refill that sock whenever it needed a little extra smell.

Chapter 11

Quick Tricks for a Scary Sitch

Try these techniques at home, and heading out will be a heck of a lot happier.

Are surprises taking the joy out of your afternoon walks? Keep these tips in your pocket to support your pup through sudden startles and out-of-nowhere scares.

Name it and tame it.
Give names to people, things, and events that scare your dog. For example, a trash truck roars down the block, slamming trash cans around as it empties them.

Step 1. Name what your dog sees as a scary monster. Let's call this one "Trash Truck."

Step 2. Feed your dog cookies while it sweeps your block. This way, you'll infuse a happier emotion into your dog and slowly chip away at their fear of the noisy truck.

The key is to feed them cookies while the trash truck is in sight and stop when it's gone, so your dog associates the scary thing with cookies. Now, when the trash truck is coming, you can announce "Trash Truck," and your dog will happily wag their tail as they await the cookies that will inevitably make their way into his mouth. Now trash trucks are fun!

Say "Ready," and you're set.
Teach a "Ready" cue (or choose any word that feels comfortable) to let
your dog know something will happen.

Step 1. Say "Ready."

Step 2. When your dog looks at you, feed them a cookie.

Do this multiple times until you see the word will encourage your dog
to look at you at least nine out of ten times. Once you have conditioned
that response, you can point something out to your dog so they aren't
surprised.

My dog is terrified of the click sound the TV makes when it turns off.
If he's napping on the floor, and I turn it off without warning, he jumps
up, wide-eyed like he was just stuck with a cattle prod. Now, I make sure
I call his name, ask him if he's ready, and then tell him I'm turning the
TV off before hitting the off button. When I give a fair warning, my dog
barely flicks an ear.

You can also use this technique as you approach a corner where
someone could suddenly appear. Try giving your "Ready" cue, and then
point to the corner. Your dog may not know what you are talking about,
but you're drawing their attention to something. That way, your dog can
gather all the information they need to be comfortable in case something
awaits them around the bend.

Cue the lift.
Sometimes it's easier to lift a dog in a scary situation. If you cue that
you're going to pick them up, you take the element of surprise out of
the equation.

Step 1. Use a combination of a verbal cue and a body position cue of
crouching down. Call your dog's name, ask them if they're ready, and
tell them that you're going to "Get vertical."

Step 2. Place your arm under their chest and through their front legs
while putting your other arm under their back end. I've practiced this
so much with my dog that when I give the "Get vertical" cue, he kicks
his back legs up onto my thigh while crouched down. In other words, he
embraces the choice to opt-in.

For practice, give your verbal cue, bend down, and place your hands in a position that will allow you to secure your dog when you lift them. Once in position, give them lots of cookies, and tell them when you're about to put them down. Giving that cue before you descend allows your dog to process what's happening.

Try different hand positions if your dog isn't happy about being picked up. Some dogs prefer your hand under their rump, so their back legs are tucked against your body. Some may want your hand under their belly with their legs dangling, while others like one hand in front and one in the back. Experiment and see what works best for your dog.

Try a lift alternative.
This is a great position to teach your dog if they're too big to lift or don't like being held.

Step 1. Start with your dog next to you, so you're both facing the same direction. Ask them to "Stay" and take a step in front of them, using your body to block them. Feed them cookies while you do this.

Step 2. After several reps, name the position or use a phrase that will describe what you are about to do. You can say, "I got this," before stepping out and body-blocking whatever's coming toward you.

Once trained in this exercise, your dog will physically relax when you step out in front of them because they know you're taking charge, which means they don't have to make any decisions. This is important for a fearful dog because they don't always make the best decisions when fear clouds their judgment.

Chapter 12

Sometimes the Decider is You

Build trust so your dog knows when "no" is best for the both of you.

Giving your dog a choice isn't always in the cards. For example, you take your dog on a walk, but you're due at work in an hour. Your dog wants to take a longer route, but you can't be late for work. In this circumstance, apologize to your dog and firmly tell them that you can't go that way today. Leave no wiggle room for negotiations.

On days when you're not pressed for time, let your dog decide the route you take. That way, on those rare occasions when you can't accommodate them, you'll have banked enough goodwill with your pup that they'll gladly comply with your wishes for that day.

There are other times when you don't feel like doing something for no valid reason other than you don't want to. You may be hot, tired, or bored of the same walk. In those instances, softly ask, "Are you sure you want to go that way?" Notice this is a different tone than when you firmly tell your dog that you need to cut your walk short so you can get to work because you should save your firm tone for those non-negotiable circumstances.

If your dog has a strong opinion, they'll stand still when you point in the other direction. If they don't have a strong opinion, they'll adjust and walk the way you want to. When their opinion strongly leans their way, turn toward your dog and walk in the direction they want. You'll be met with a happy pup whose bounce in that direction is all you need to know that it was important to them that you go their way.

This isn't some elaborate communication method that's beyond your reach. It's about a simple give-and-take relationship that creates deep trust and respect between you and your dog. The trick is consistency, patience, and lots and lots of love.

Photo courtesy of Unsplash - Angel Moya Perona

Wait for the Wings to Flutter

The transformation is worth the wait and more beautiful than you can imagine.

While this book provides tools to help you and your dog in certain situations, the real work occurs in your everyday interactions and your philosophical approach to treating your dog like the canine citizen they are. Your dog isn't a robot without feelings. They are a living, feeling creature who probably thinks they hit the lottery when they met you.

If you're reading this book, you're open to the *Confident by Choice* approach and the small steps it takes to spark incredible change. Edward Lorenz, a meteorologist at MIT, noticed that a small change can have far-reaching consequences. He said that the flap of a butterfly's wings could ultimately cause a tornado, and "The Butterfly Effect" was born. This concept isn't limited to the weather. I've seen it in dog training over and over again.

All of the subtle actions we take can profoundly impact any dog. For example, giving the dog access to a door can lead to a strong sense of confidence. Letting them choose which direction to take on a hike builds resilience over time. A kind word or scratch behind the ears can be the seed of an unbreakable relationship between you and your dog. Don't underestimate the power of these small yet ever-significant things.

You have the tools to take your dog from cautious to confident. Start today by observing, giving your dog a vote, and tailoring *Confident by Choice* to support and celebrate your dog's personality. If you'd like to share your progress, I'd love to hear it. Feel free to reach out to me at wagmoreu@gmail.com.

Photo by M. Nicole Fischer Photography

Resources

Check out these resources to gain even more inspiration.

Online Resources

Amy Cook, Ph.D., founder and creator of The Play Way:
www.playwaydogs.com

Fenzi Dog Sports Academy Classes (www.fenzidogsportsacademy.com)
  • Dealing with the Bogeyman: Helping Fearful and Reactive
    and Stressed Dogs
  • Working with Reactive and Hyper-Aroused Dogs

Sharon Carroll: http://www.avantidogtraining.com.au

Debbie Jacobs, CPDT-KA, CAP, Author and Canine Behavior Specialist:
www.fearfuldogs.com

Nicole Wilde, CPDT, Author and Canine Behavior Specialist:
www.nicolewilde.com

Books

General Behavior
The Other End Of The Leash by Patricia B. McConnell, Ph.D.
Bones Would Rain from the Sky by Suzanne Clothier

Fearful Behavior
A Guide To Living With & Training A Fearful Dog by Debbie Jacobs,
CPDT-KA, CAP
Help For Your Fearful Dog by Nicole Wilde, CPDT

Canine Body Language
*Canine Body Language - A Photographic Guide, Interpreting the Native
Language of the Domestic Dog* by Brenda Aloff
On Talking Terms with Dogs: Calming Signals by Turid Rugaas

Stress in Dogs
Stress, Anxiety and Aggression in Dogs by Anders Hallgren
*Stress in Dogs – Learn how dogs show stress and what you can do to
help* by Martina Scholz & Clarissa von Reinhardt

About the Author

Stacey Manzo holds several designations and certifications, including CPDT-KA, CPCFT, Reiki Master, AKC Canine Good Citizen Evaluator, Certified Trick Dog Instructor, and others. She began teaching group dog training classes in 2005 and hasn't stopped since. Stacey believes in working with the whole dog through training, behavior management, emotional support, and physical fitness. She has studied under top trainers and continues to leverage cutting-edge new approaches to working with dogs as science and discovery evolve.